My First Team

I0806817

GYMNASTICS

by KIM THOMPSON

TABLE OF CONTENTS

A Pelican Book

SEAHORSE PUBLISHING

Teaching Tips for Caregivers and Teachers:

Research shows that one of the best ways for students to learn a new topic is to read about it.

Before Reading

- Read the title and predict what the book will be about.
- Read the "Words to Know" and discuss the meaning of each word.
- Read the back cover to see what the book is about.

During Reading

- When a student gets to a word that is unknown, ask them to look at the rest of the sentence to find clues to help with the meaning of the unknown word.
- Motivate students with praise and encouragement.

After Reading

- Discuss the main idea of the book.
- Ask students to give one detail that they learned in the book.

SIGHT WORDS

a
again
and
are
can
do
down
jump
up
we

WORDS TO KNOW

balance

bend

gymnastics

roll

team

gymnastics

We do **gymnastics.**

We can **bend**.

bend

balance

We can **balance**.

We jump up and down.

We **roll** again and again.

roll

We are a gymnastics **team**!

team

Index

Written by: Kim Thompson
Design by: Jen Bowers
Series Development: James Earley

Photos: cover and bottom of p.9 ©2019 Anatoliy Karlyuk/Shutterstock; p.4-5 ©2014 Sasha Samardzija/Shutterstock; p.6 ©2016 Svitlana Bezuhlova/Shutterstock, ©2019 marina_eno1/Shutterstock; p.7 ©2016 Garry0305/Shutterstock; p.8 ©2019 Erickson Stock/Shutterstock; p.9 ©2018 Master1305/Shutterstock; p.10-11 ©2014 d13/Shutterstock; p.13 ©2016 Kaderov Andrii/Shutterstock; p.15 ©2020 Vladimir Vasiltvich/Shutterstock

Library of Congress PCN Data
Gymnastics / Kim Thompson
My First Team
ISBN 978-1-63897-421-5 (hard cover)
ISBN 978-1-63897-536-6 (paperback)
ISBN 978-1-63897-651-6 (EPUB)
ISBN 978-1-63897-766-7 (eBook)
Library of Congress Control Number: 2021953264

Printed in the United States of America.

Seahorse Publishing Company
www.seahorsepub.com

Published in the United States
Seahorse Publishing
PO Box 771325
Coral Springs, FL 33077

SEAHORSE PUBLISHING